Beyond Survival

How to Turn Survival Into Financial
Freedom

By: Saundra R. Gage

Table of Contents

Acknowledgments

Many people helped make this book a reality. Without them, it would have been almost impossible to complete this project. It is my pleasure to thank them here.

Special Thanks to Lisa Nichols and Motivating the Masses team for inspiring me to write and release the story on the inside of me that has been hidden for so long.

Thank you to Kidd Marketing for your ongoing assistance and encouragement in the birth of this book.

Chelsey Marie created the beautiful cover design and layout. Thanks, Chelsey Marie.

Thank you Cassandra Campbell, of Cassandra's So Glam Photography for the beautiful photograph on the front cover of my book.

Finally, I give special thanks to my support team: my two daughters Shanda and Lakesha, my son-in-love, Carlos Hudgins and my brother Robert Woolbright for their constant encouragement and support throughout this project. Also, I want to thank my sisters Deloris Harris and Bonnie Capers and my friend Cassandra Campbell for their encouragement.

Introduction

First of all, let me applaud you for picking up this book because I know all of us tend to put off our finances until we absolutely have no other choice but to face them. So good for you, for taking the bull by the horns and really truly addressing how you can handle your finances better. What I want you to know is that your finances are a game. Most of us have never been taught the rules of that game, and so we struggle. However, that struggle doesn't have to continue. Once you know how that game is played, what the rules of the game are, and some strategies to be able to win at the financial game, you can feel confident and boldly, assertively, handle your finances in a powerful way that may seem scary to you right now. I promise you, in the end, you'll be glad you did.

For some of you, it may even be a little bit

of fun. So, as we go through this book together, know that I'm here for you; that I know what it's like to have problems with and even fears around your finances. But I can also tell you that once you feel in control of them, it's a freedom that you'll be glad you took the time to invest in yourself. One last thing before we get into it, I want you to know, that no matter what your bank account says, you are valuable. Your self-worth has nothing to do with your net worth.

Thriving Beyond the Past

When I look at my life today, I realize how blessed I am because I found my voice. I have found that there is power in discovering your own voice. I am learning to speak up for myself. I will never be silenced, again. I'm finally free to be the person I was always meant to be. As I look in the mirror at myself, I see a woman who has succeeded in everything that she has put her mind to. I see how much she has accomplished, no matter where she served. I have had a successful career in the federal government for thirty years, twenty-eight of which were with NASA Glenn Research Center, the National Aeronautics Space Administration. During my career, I have been recognized multiple times for my work and dedication. I have received the Grant Specialist of the Year Award twice, and I have received one of the highest

NASA awards, the Exceptional Service Medal, right before I retired in 2015.

I am a woman who always serves with love and care and excellence; it has always been my goal to leave a space better than it was before I entered that space. My focus has always been on doing my very best, and I never had to ask to be recognized or promoted because of my service and work ethic. As a change agent, I seek to find the truth in a situation so that I can come up with solutions that will allow others to work smarter and not harder.

Today, I am living a life of financial freedom because I know how to master my personal finances through self-control, self-discipline, and commitment. I have learned to trust myself and ignore the constant distractions that would cause me to lose focus on my goals and my desires. I have been able to look deeper into things and find the strategies and methods to solve problems. I can look beyond what the masses are doing and see the best strategy for change.

Surviving Life in the Past

What you probably don't know about me is that it hasn't always been this way. I am one of four daughters. I never knew my father and barely knew my mother. My grandmother raised me until her passing when I was twelve years old. I met my mother for the first time when she came to her mother's funeral. Then she asked me if I wanted to live with her. I did because I wanted to know who she was. So, I went to live with my mother until I was 15. During that time that I stayed with her, she was in and out of the hospital, until she passed away from tuberculosis.

I then went to live with my oldest sister. I stayed with my sister, her husband, and her daughter until I was engaged to be married at eighteen years old. About two weeks after I graduated high school, I moved to San Diego, California, where I married my husband who was a sailor in the US Navy. I had one child in this marriage. For two years, I did as I was told. I didn't question anything. I didn't feel I had any power and I definitely didn't have a voice of my own. I just accepted my plight in the hope that if I did everything as I was told, that he would love me as I loved him. Unfortunately, it didn't work out that way. No matter what I did, I never received what I was giving.

I found myself on this roller coaster ride. Doing this and then doing that, but it was never enough. There were days I was just surviving from day to day, not knowing how I was going to make it or where my next meal was coming from. To make the situation worse; I was pregnant. While I was in this physical state, I couldn't even think about dreaming. I was alone a lot because my husband decided when and if he wanted to come home. I had no family close by to support or help me. Somehow, I survived even though I was malnourished. I gave birth to my daughter prematurely, after which, things only got worse. I had to leave after two and a half years into the marriage because of physical abuse. My 14-month-old daughter and I secretly got a ride to the airport, and I flew to Ohio to live with another sister.

Four years later, I married again and had two more children. During this marriage, I felt emotionally abused, neglected, and right back on that roller coaster ride again. No matter what I did, it didn't turn out the way I hoped it would. Then I was hurt and disappointed as I dealt with my husband's infidelity. So, eventually, I divorced him as well. It was at this point that I realized that I had to stop looking for someone else to love me or take care of me. I had to do what I needed to do. I couldn't depend on anyone else to do it. After all, I have been abandoned, neglected, and I have escaped sexual abuse, twice. I survived two divorces, starvation, physical abuse and emotional abuse. I realize that the things I experienced in my past cannot define me or keep me from being who God created me to be. In spite of the things that were meant to destroy me physically, mentally and emotionally, I was still standing. I decided to fight for a better life.

I took the reins. I stopped looking for people to see me and hear me. I no longer allowed the response of people to determine who I was or what I was going to do. I became determined to fight any obstacles that might get in my way. I had to move beyond survival and become the person I needed to be for my children's sake. It was at this point that I realized that I had to have the tenacity, the drive and the will to do more and to be more. I was so used to other people making decisions for me; I was so used to being silent in spite of what I wanted or how I felt. During my two marriages, my voice was pretty silent.

In my first marriage, I had no voice. Every time I would speak up, I was beaten down so I learned to be quiet because it was hard to know what might set him off if I were to speak up. I moved far away from all my friends and family, so I had no one to support me in any way. I felt like I was in captivity. I was not allowed to have friends or go anywhere but to work and then home. I had no say in our finances or any decisions that were made for that matter. In fact, I had no control over anything. I thought we didn't have much money, if any. We could barely pay the rent and often I was hungry because there was no food to eat. There were decisions that my husband made that did not make any sense. For example, on one occasion my husband left in his car to go to the naval base, but that evening, he returned in a new car, that he decided to purchase without consulting me at all.

In my second marriage, it appeared that I had a say in some of the decisions that were made but, when I think about it, I know it only appeared that way. I was often responsible for handling the finances. I would budget our money and determine which bills needed to be paid at which time. I would always ask my husband to sit down to review what I had done so we would be in agreement. This was completely pointless because I could never get him to understand that just because the bank statement or the ATM had a balance, it wasn't necessarily the actual balance that was available. So, after I spent so much time preparing a budget, reviewing the bills and writing the checks, my husband would just often go to the ATM machine and withdraw money to buy some new tires or some other thing he decided he wanted. I can't tell you how frustrated I was when the non-sufficient fund notices or overdraft fees came in the mail. It put us further in the hole because we had to pay overdraft fees with money we really didn't have. I was desperate for a solution to my dilemma.

I tried everything from giving him some bills to be responsible for while I kept the most important bills, like rent and utilities. It still didn't work. I realize that when people are desperate, they make mistakes that affect their finances and keep them from being successful in life. I have had two marriages and have had to file chapter 13 bankruptcies twice. Why am I sharing this information? Because I realized that, after my second marriage, that you cannot spend more than you earn continually and think that it won't eventually catch up with you.

It was as if I was in a deep, deep, sleep that I couldn't wake up from. I was stuck in this continuous cycle. But something happened, one day, I woke up and I made up my mind that things had to change. I didn't know it then, but I now realize that your state of mind (your mindset) is the ink in the pen that writes your life story.

When I look back at my life, I was so busy trying to please other people to get the things I felt I was missing in my life (like the love of my mother and grandmother, the father I never knew, my sisters, a brother that no one knows who he is, where he is, or if he ever existed, and even the love of two husbands). I was willing to do almost anything. I was willing to lose myself for just a little love, attention, and validation. I gave so much and received very little in return. I was killing me and I didn't even know it. I wasn't the person I was created to be, I was the person everyone else wanted me to be. I wasted many years of my life afraid of displeasing the people I loved. But the moment the real me spoke up or stood up I was often abandoned or punished for it, so I quietly would retreat to the little me. My heart was beating and the blood was rushing through my veins but I was really dead on the inside. Was I brain dead? I might as well have been because it was if I was sleep walking through my life, unaware of what I was doing to the real me on the inside. It wasn't until I separate and divorced my second husband that I began to slowly come out of this sleep walking stupor. It was this crisis that jolted me awake and into reality. When I woke up I had to deal with the reality of my situation so I assessed where I was physically, mentally, emotionally, and financially and then I made a conscious, committed decision to do whatever it takes to change my life. But I must tell you I had a really big why behind my decision. If your why is big enough, you will be strong enough and determined enough to push through every obstacle that happens to get in your way.

My big why is and always will be my children. I didn't want them to go through the things I have gone through. I made it all about them and then I found the real me in the process. I didn't realize it at the time but I was operating in a scarcity mindset. I was afraid that people would abandon me or wouldn't love me back. When you are stuck in a limiting belief you cannot see or accept possibilities or opportunities even if they are right in front of you. If you are stuck in an endless cycle, you may be like I was…one of the walking dead or sleep walking through your life. Well, it's time to wake up sleeping beauty! It's time to wake up the sleeping giant! This is your wakeup call! Shake yourself! Take a moment and find a place where you won't be disturbed. Take this time to really, really, think about your life. This is your responsibility! You have to be your own rescue and it all starts with pushing beyond your limiting beliefs and negative mindsets that are embedded and so deeply ingrained in your mind that you have become frozen in the status quo where you are comfortable. You must make a choice to bust out of your comfort zone and wakeup the person you are meant to become. Wake up and come out of this captivity so you can move beyond where you are and into the life you were always meant to live.

New Perspectives:
An Empowering Journey

Many of my life experiences of the past were not what I wanted or dreamed, but I am sure that it has made me into the person I am today! It has helped me to empower myself and to stand in my truth. As a single mother, I am thankful that I have a new perspective in life. I am thankful that my life's journey, my goals, dreams, and plans have brought me to a place in life where I cannot only plan and dream and have goals and find my purpose in this life, but, I am able to pursue it with all my heart. I am thankful that I have learned real strategies that have taught me how to master my finances, how to finally be in control.

I've learned how to be the master of my mind and my thoughts regardless of what I have experienced in my life. If you want to win the game you have to either know the rules or change the rules so that the rules are in your favor. I have been able to change the game, and learn the rules around this economic system. I am the master of my situation, and I no longer allow the outside environment or people to dictate my life. I have learned that if I live beneath my means, I will have money to save for my future needs and desires. I have learned that you cannot avoid creditors and bill collectors. If you have obtained a loan of any kind, you have signed a promissory note that you will pay back the money plus interest. I have also learned that if you really want to win the game of money, you have to understand how it works. You have to know the rules so that you can play to win.

I realize that so many people don't know the rules. They are just making it up as they go along. If our parents didn't know the rules, and the school systems are not really teaching us the rules, we just make up the rules based on what we see other people doing until we realize that we don't know what we are doing.

When I decided to improve my financial education by researching everything I could about how to win at personal finances, things began to turn around. I went to college for accounting, business management and have worked for the federal government in accounting, financial management, grant management and contract management. I have worked as the treasurer of a small church and served on the Board of Directors as a treasurer for a large church. All these experiences have given me a lot of insight into financial management. As an independent single mother, I use my skills and abilities to get all my personal finances under control. At one point, I was able to pay off all my bills except my mortgage. The reason I didn't pay off my mortgage, is because it was not in my reduction plan. But now, I am the master of my finances because I am living in the overflow. I am able to move forward with many opportunities that are bringing me closer to my goals.

The solution that I found that worked best is to really know your net worth as well as your self-worth. Your net worth is your total assets minus your total liabilities or debt. Your self-worth is the value you place on yourself. Make excellence your goal for everything you do. See yourself winning in every situation. Pursue excellence with all your might. If you work excellently on the job, it will not go unnoticed. Living an excellent kind of life will cause you to be lifted up. Stop looking at your flaws and look at your strengths. You become what you focus on the most. You have to know that you are a valuable individual. Never let anyone convince you that you have no value. No one will value you until you value yourself. There is greatness in you because you were created to do great things. It is up to you to continually let that greatness come out. See yourself as the person you want to be.

We are what we think we are. If we think we are wealthy, we are wealthy. If we think we are living in poverty, we will. If you want to be wealthy, do what the wealthy do. You can walk in wealth by acting and speaking wealth every day. Find wealthy people and make them your mentor. If you can't personally sit down with them for an interview, spend time researching them. Find out everything you can about them. This is the quickest way to get where you want to be. You have to stop that old poverty mentality from taking over your life. A person with a poverty mentality keeps doing all the wrong things. At the top of the list is the things that you say. Don't keep rehearsing the things you see. Instead, rehearse the things you want to see. You create your world by the things that you say. Don't constantly talk about your struggle, talk about your blessings. You need to know and understand what your limiting beliefs are about money. You need to identify what you have been taught about money from your family, friends and through your experiences. How do you feel about money? It is important to bring your thoughts and feelings about money to the forefront so that you can identify where you are now and assess where you need to change the way you think about money. To change your mindset means you will have to make a change in your lifestyle to implement the change of mind. Giving up what you normally do may seem like you are depriving yourself of something that brought you pleasure but you have to look at it as a sacrifice for something better.

Deprivation has a negative connotation. You are not changing your mindset for negative purposes but for positive purposes. When you decide to give up excessive spending to get your spending under control and improve your financial standing that is a positive, not negative outcome. This is a sacrifice that you have decided to make because you have truly changed your mind about how you spend money. If you have not really changed your mind, you will perceive every attempt to stop overspending as depriving you of what you really want to do.

The Journey to Financial Freedom

What is your financial health status? Determining your net worth will give you a snapshot of your financial health. Money is just a tool that you use to get the things that you need, want and desire. It is important to know the rules of money so that you can make money work for you and not you work for money.

The number one solution to improving your financial health is to save more money than you spend. Always pay yourself first. Make savings a priority in your life. Learn to keep more than you earn, and you will have money available to save and invest in your future. You must have a plan to be financially successful. If you don't plan to save and invest, you will spend every dime that you make. You have to be willing to change your mindset into a financially healthy state of mind and being.

If you want the solution to work, you will have to change your previous financial behaviors to be more consistent with the behavior that is needed to obtain and maintain a financially fit life.

It will take work and determination to resolve your financial situation. You have to make changes on purpose to see the results that you are looking for. You need to know exactly what is going on with your finances so you must track everything that is coming in and everything that is going out. You should know your credit history and your credit score. It is your responsibility to know your financial state so that you can make the adjustments whenever they are needed.

If you stay on top of your finances, you will not be caught by too many surprises. In regards to surprises, you should also determine the areas that you need to set aside funding to cover the replacement of cars, appliances or cover expenses during a time of unemployment. Then, you will have money available to cover those expenses and will not have to use credit unexpectedly.

I remember the first time I moved into my own apartment. I worked for the telephone company, and I barely made minimum wage. I lived in my apartment with my three-year-old daughter; I said it was an apartment, but it wasn't really. I lived in Oberlin Ohio which is a college town. I rented two rooms for $80.00 a month. It was a house that was also being rented by college students. I had to share the bathroom and kitchen with the college students living there.

After taxes and my car payment were taken out of my check, I barely had enough to pay the rent, buy food and put gas in the car. It was during this time that I learned how important it was to manage your money. I needed to know where every dime went. If you want to feel more in control of your finances, then you have to take the time to track your money. Track everything that is coming in which is income, and everything that is going out, which are expenses. You cannot turn a blind eye to what is happening in your finances and think that it will all work itself out in the end because it won't.

In order to be financially fit and well, you need to know what is on your credit report and your credit score. Just as you receive a grade report on your academic history, you have a credit report based on your credit history. Whereas, academically you received your GPA based on your grades in school, you also are graded on how you handle your credit and receive a credit score. You should always know how you are doing credit-wise. You need to know your credit history to determine what you need to adjust as well as making sure that creditors are reporting your information correctly.

Once, I requested my credit report, and I found a medical bill for a hospital that I had not visited in years. I contacted the credit bureau to dispute the charge, and they did their investigation. Weeks later the credit bureau responded that the charge was correct and that they would not be removing this from my credit report. Well, I knew that it was not my charge, so I called them. They insisted that it was correct, but the information that I found out indicated to me that the medical bill was my daughter's medical bill and not mine. You see, her name is Shanda and my name is Saundra. The names are similar but not the same.

I informed the credit bureau of this, but

they wouldn't budge. They did give me the contact information to the credit collection agency that was handling it. I called them, and they argued with me that it was my bill and just didn't believe me when I told them that it was my daughter who had my granddaughter in that hospital during that time. To make a long story short, I finally had to tell the credit collection agency and the credit bureau that I was going to report this to the government organization that was responsible for policing the credit bureaus and credit collection agencies. After I threatened to turn them in, they took a closer look at the situation and realized that I was right because I did not have the same social security number as my daughter. Finally, they removed the information from my credit report. So, I guess it is not a good idea to name your daughter with a name that could be confused with your own.

It is crucial to review your credit history to make sure that your credit information is reported correctly and that you are not a victim of identity fraud or theft. Stay on top of your finances so that you know immediately when things are not consistent with what you have been doing. You also need to watch your credit score even if you are not currently thinking of obtaining any credit. Your credit score is a good indicator of how you are handling your credit.

As a result of my financial wellness coaching, you will decrease your financial stress significantly and feel more in control while embracing peace through financial freedom. For the person who desires to leave the 9 to 5 job to become an entrepreneur and pursue a full-time business one day, it is important to achieve financial freedom in your personal finances so you can successfully manage your business finances. Financial freedom is the key to your financial abundance no matter where your income falls on the pay scale. If you don't have control of your personal finances now, you will not have control of your business finances in the future.

As a young married person, I had to teach myself by trial and error how to handle my finances. It is almost impossible to maintain financial health and wellness when married couples are not on the same page regarding the financial decisions that need to be made. No one told me that I shouldn't spend more than I earn. No one told me that it would be even more difficult to manage your finances when each person in the marriage had different plans for how the money should be spent.

My ex-husband and I had this dance around finances every time we got paid. I would budget the money, and he would spend the money that we did not have budgeted. Eventually, things got so bad that we had to file for a chapter 13. After we paid back all our debts, we finally had the opportunity to get a house. We got the house and slowly, over time, our financial situation started to get right back into the same problems.

I tried everything from separating the bills between us to having two separate checking accounts, one in his name, and one in my name. I soon realized that you have to be on the same page as the other person. You both have to really want to get your finances under control for it to actually happen. It doesn't matter that you were not taught in the past how to handle your finances. With all the information and technology available today, all you really need is the willingness to change where you are. You have to make a decision and then take the necessary action to turn your situation around.

In May of 1992, I became a single mother. I was determined to come out of this vicious cycle of debt. I read everything I could get my hands on. I worked diligently to pay off the debt that I had. Eventually, I was successful at paying off all my debt except my mortgage. During this process, I have learned to look at debt and strategize how to reduce it or eliminate it. You should never let debt control you. You must always be on top of the situation and really know and understand every aspect of your debt. I learned that all debt is not bad. You just have to know the rules, so you know how to play the game.

I retired with 30 years of federal government service. As an employee of the federal government, I had the opportunity to contribute to the Thrift Savings Plan, which is the government's version of the private sector's 401K. Unfortunately, I did not make extra contributions to the plan until the last fifteen years of my career. As part of the Thrift Savings Plan, the government matches up to 5% of an employee's contribution. This means that I left a lot of money on the table. Also, in the latter years of my career, I could have made additional payments into the plan even though the government would not match the funds.

I wish that I would have contributed to my Thrift Savings Plan at the beginning of my career and that I would have contributed the extra payments near the end of my career. If I had contributed more, my Thrift Savings Plan retirement account balance would have been much greater by the time I retired. If I contributed 5% of my salary into the Thrift Savings Plan when I started with the federal government, I would have also received the 5% matching contributions from the government over thirty years of my employment. This means my plan balance would have been much higher than it was. This also means that I would have had a lot more money available when I retired. I could have used the additional money to fund my business or to build my dream home. The additional money would have given me the ability to do more in retirement.

I wish I knew then what I know now. When I think about my jobs and career over the years, my goal was always about how much money they would pay me. I never really thought about the benefits. Twenty years before I retired from the federal government I realized that benefits are just as important as money. I always considered how much money I would get and if an employer had good health and dental coverage because I had kids, but I never really looked beyond that.

I found that jobs that offered educational

benefits allowed me to pursue my continuing education. I was looking for ways to pay for college, but I never thought about retirement benefits. I worked at Oberlin College for about four years, but it was through a grant with the Office of Education. I didn't realize that Oberlin College was automatically contributing money into a TIAA retirement account on my behalf until I left the position. I don't know if Oberlin College offered a match for my contribution and I don't remember anyone telling me I could contribute money to my TIAA retirement account. I probably received the paperwork when I was hired, but because I was so young, I probably didn't pay attention to it.

When I went to work for the federal government, I knew that they had the Thrift Saving Plan. I knew that the federal government automatically contributed 1% of my salary to the plan and I knew that they would match any contributions that I put into the plan up to 5% but I didn't contribute anything until 15 years before my retirement. I was struggling to meet my family expenses, so I only contributed a small amount of my salary to be matched. As I really looked at the benefits of contributing to the Thrift Savings Plan, I increased my contribution to 5% maybe ten years before I retired. I am not saying that I didn't have a nice sum in my plan when I retired, but I am saying that I left a lot of money on the table. When you contribute to a Thrift Savings Plan or a 401(k) that is matched by your employer that is like FREE MONEY! If I had fully contributed up to the 5% match, I would have had about four times the amount in my account when I retired.

The federal government recently changed the way they onboard new employees. When I was hired, we were given the option to contribute to the Thrift Savings Plan; now, the only option is to OPT-OUT. The federal government automatically assumes you want to contribute at least 1% of your salary. You have to actually say you do not want to contribute to the Thrift Savings Plan. I wish that this rule was in place when I got hired. The earlier you contribute towards your retirement, the better. I know that retirement is the furthest thing from your mind when you are looking for a job to support you and/or your family but the earlier you start saving towards retirement, the more you will have to sustain you in the lifestyle you want to live when you retire. Also, the money that you contribute to your plan or 401(k) is contributed with pre-tax dollars. It doesn't really affect your net pay that much.

What I wish I did sooner. As with most young people, when I came to the government I was a young married person with children. My thoughts were centered around meeting my family's current needs. I didn't think about retirement because I was too involved with making ends meet and providing for my family.

In 1997, a coworker encouraged me to begin to contribute to the Thrift Savings Plan. She even talked about how I was missing the opportunity to get my contributions matched by the government. Even though it was hard to grasp how important this was, I followed her advice and started to contribute a small portion of my salary into the Thrift Savings Plan. However, I didn't contribute the 5%. I ended up settling on about 2% at that time. When I did this, I realized that this contribution was with pre-tax dollars and that my contribution of pre-tax dollars did not really affect my net income as much as I thought it would.

I didn't contribute the 5% percent because I didn't think I could afford to decrease my net pay that much. I went on this way for at least five years. As my salary increased, I began to increase the amount I contributed. I kept this up until I finally reached the 5% contribution. I probably kept it at the 5% contribution level until the financial crisis hit.

For about three years after the financial crisis, government salaries were frozen, so there were no annual raises. Everyone was getting a bailout but government workers had to tighten their belts. Our annual salary stayed the same while our expenses continued to climb. To make ends meet I had to lower my Thrift Savings Plan contribution. All during the recession, I heard fellow employees wondering if they were going to be able to retire at all because they were dipping into their Thrift Savings Plan, trying to stay afloat. I realized now that I would have been in a better position for retirement if I had started my 5% contribution to the Thrift Savings Plan from day one of my employment. When you contribute to a 401(k) or Thrift Saving Plan with pre-tax dollars your take-home pay is not reduced by the actual amount you contribute to the retirement plan. For example, if you were in the state of Ohio, and you had an annual salary of $50,000 and elected to contribute 5% of your biweekly salary, the amount that would be contributed to your 401(k) or Thrift Savings Plan retirement account would be $96 while your estimated net pay would be reduced by $69. If you decided only to contribute 2% of your biweekly salary, the amount that would be contributed into your 401(k) or Thrift Savings Plan retirement account would be $38 while your estimated net pay would be reduced by $28. If you had an annual salary of $100,000 and elected to contribute 5% of your biweekly salary, the amount that would be contributed into your 401(k) or Thrift Savings Plan retirement account would be $192 while your estimated net pay would be reduced by $138. If you decided to contribute 2% of your biweekly salary, the amount that would be contributed into your 401(k) or Thrift Savings Plan retirement account would be $77 while your estimated net pay would be reduced by $55.

Steps to Financial Freedom

Action Step One: Assess Your Financial Health. You can't fix what you don't know is broken. You should take the time to assess the state of your financial health often. Just as you need to have a physical check-up to determine that you are in good health, you should also take the time to assess your financial well-being periodically. Two of the obvious tools you should tap into is your credit report and your credit score. You need to request your credit report. How do you know that the amount of debt that you think you have is the amount of debt showing on your credit report? It is your responsibility to monitor your credit. You can get a free credit report from the three credit reporting agencies; Equifax, Experian, and Trans Union, annually from www.annualcreditreport.com. You can also request your credit score for a fee, or you can check out Credit Karma to get a free credit score.

When assessing your financial health and wellness, you need to ask yourself several questions to diagnose how you are doing. Here are several questions to ask: Does your income exceed your expenses? Do you know your net worth? Is your net worth positive or negative? Are you tracking your income and expenses? Do you use a spending plan? Are you paying all your bills on time? Do you save more than you spend? Are you paying yourself first? Do you have an emergency fund to cover unexpected expenses? Are you saving for retirement? What is your financial stress level? Low? Medium? High? Non-existent? Are you confident that you can make an informed financial decision?

Action Step Two: Determine Your

Money Mindset. How do you feel about money? Who told you how to handle your financial life? Do you think of money positively or negatively? You need to understand that money is a tool to get you what you need, want and desire. It all depends on how you developed your relationship with money. If you grew up in a state of lack and scarcity, you might look at money as hard to get and hard to keep. If you grew up in a state of abundance, you might look at money as something you always had and expect to continue to have in the future. How you think about money affects how you handle and manage your money.

You can develop your money mindset from your family, friends and the environment you live in. You need to understand how you think about money because it determines your financial behavior. You need to understand that you have to master your money so that your money does not master you. When you understand the rules of money, you will know how to play the game.

Action Step Three: Set Your Financial Goals. After you assess your financial health, you need to set financial goals. You cannot leave anything to chance. If there is something you want to accomplish and it is going to take money to get it done, you need to set a financial goal showing how you are going to accomplish it. You should set several financial goals because you need to give your money purpose, so it knows where it is supposed to go.

Be intentional about your money. If you want to purchase a home or car, you should set financial goals to accomplish those purchases. You should also set savings as one of your financial goals. Identify all the things that you need to save for and provide the action steps you plan to take to accomplish those goals. So whatever your financial goals are you need to write them down and establish the action steps you will take and the dates when you expect to accomplish those action steps.

Action Step Four: Develop A Strategic Plan For Financial Health. Financial well-being doesn't just happen; you have to plan for it strategically. What's your strategy? You must have a strategy to get your finances under control. You need a solid strategy and plan to be financially successful. Temperance and control are necessary for any changes you make. People often attempt to change some aspect of their life, but as time goes on, they resume their former behaviors. To break bad habits, you have to replace them with good habits and practice the good habits until they become permanent. Otherwise, you will return to your bad habits again. There are several plans that you need to put in place to make sure that you reach your financial health goals. You need to develop a spending plan. I personally believe that a spending plan is better than a budget. There are many negative connotations with the word "budget." Because a budget is considered to be constricting, people don't follow the budget they have created. A spending plan is developed based on the results of your financial assessment. Identify all income and expenses.Then, you track all your expenses for thirty days.

Do you know where all your money is going? Your credit card statement will only list the things that you charge on your card. What about those expenses that you pay with cash? Do you know how much money is falling through the cracks? Instead of creating a budget with estimates of what you think you might spend, you plan how much you want to spend in each category. You may find that some expenses are not really serving your financial goals. A spending plan is better than a budget because you are planning what you will spend in each category. A spending plan is felt to be more flexible than a budget because if you spend less than you plan you can just adjust your spending plan and move the overage of funds not used to another category.

Action Step Five: Financial Tracking Systems. One of the most important things you can do is track your finances. You need to either create or find a system that can track all the financial categories you want to monitor and track so that you can stay on top of your financial situation. To stay financially healthy, you need to consistently track all money coming in, your income and all money going out your expenses. You can manually create your own system in a spreadsheet or a table in Microsoft Word, or you can check out ready-made money management software systems like Quicken, etc. Whatever you choose to track your finances, you need to set aside time to analyze your finances at least once a month.

I prefer to review and analyze my finances at least twice a month. Technology is so wonderful. Today, almost every financial institution gives you the ability to access and review your account online. You can review your balances and transfer funds from your checking to saving and/or to loans that you have with that financial institution. You can monitor and track payments as they clear your checking account. This is a great benefit because you can look at your account balance every day if you want to. Before you had to wait until you received your bank statement. Now, you no longer have to wait for the bank statement to reconcile your checking account. You can reconcile checking account every day if you want to.

Most creditors and utility companies also give you the ability to access and review your statement online as well as pay your account online. When you track your income and expenses, you will feel more in control of your finances. You will be able to make confident financial decisions because you will know your financial status.

Action Step Six: Maintaining Financial Health and Wellness. Saving money is one of the most important elements to maintain your financial health. Saving money is the key to financial freedom. If you want to break away from the payday to payday cycle find some money to save. The more you save, the better. If you can only save one dollar, you should save that dollar. Saving money for that rainy day will be your life saver and will keep you from overspending and charging your credit cards. I want to say it again because if you capture this secret "savings is key," you will soar financially. Be sure to focus more on saving than spending. Try not to go into debt to grow your dream. When you live in financial freedom, you have the ability to consider opportunities because you are no longer constrained by financial lack. To obtain and maintain financial health and wellness, you must adequately build up your savings. Save for the things you want rather than going into debt to get them. You end up paying way more for that item than you need to when you go into debt for it too. Saving something every time you receive money, helps you create a savings habit. Savings works for you while debt works against you. Why don't people save more? If you put saving at the bottom of your list, you will never have enough leftover to save. Those who strive to save something even the smallest amount is in a better place than those who save nothing. I encourage you to pursue financial freedom as your ultimate goal. This goal is obtainable so reach for it. When you have financial freedom, you are not bound by debt. You are free to do what you want to do. When you walk in financial freedom, you do not miss opportunities because you have the money to pursue them.

Living beneath your means is absolutely necessary to get ahead. If you spend all the income that you receive, you will never get ahead. When you live below your means or income, you have money left to save and invest. You can't achieve living below your means without tracking your income and expenses. You need to know exactly what's coming in and what's going out. For some reason, we want to live like a free agent and just spend, spend, spend until it is gone and hope and believe that everything will be covered for the month. This is not good stewardship. You must take control over your money, or it will surely take control of you. Most people don't realize that if they would have self-discipline and control over their finances now that in the future they will have more freedom to purchase the things they want and need without worrying about the price. It takes the willingness to step out of the box that you have put yourself into and no longer operating as other people do. Breaking away is not always easy. I did because I didn't have a choice. It may seem that you are depriving yourself, but instead, you are building your financial future in such a way that you will be free to buy what you want when you want it. When you have control of your finances, you are in a position to build wealth, and you are in a position to pursue your dreams. You will be in a better position to help others when you take this step to help yourself. You cannot help someone else when you are struggling to make ends meet. You cannot leave the security of your 9 to 5 job to pursue that full-time business you want to build when you don't have control of your personal finances. You must stay strong and forge ahead so that you can reap the reward of your efforts. The key is to always live beneath your means by never spending more than you earn. Monitor and track your income and expenses on a consistent basis so that you know everything that is happening with your finances. Make sure you keep your emergency fund adequately funded to cover any unexpected expenses.

Review and analyze your financial status quarterly: by checking on your net worth, and your credit utilization ratio. Request your credit report, annually at the very least, and keep an eye on your credit score. Based on what you find you should make any necessary adjustments.

At least once a month review the progress that you are making towards your financial goals. You may also want to develop a savings plan. Think about the things you want to save for and then determine how much and how often you are going to put money into your savings plan. You will also need to establish an emergency fund. Expenses fall into several categories: Fixed, Variable, Known and Unknown. You can plan for your known expenses very easily, but you must also assume that there will be some unknown expenses. Expect the unexpected. Are you prepared to handle that unexpected event that happens in your life? Are you convinced that everything will stay the same every day? We are so relaxed in our everyday lives that we don't think about the possibility of change. Life happens, and things do change. Sometimes the change is a good experience and sometimes it is bad. We cannot control everything, but we can be prepared for some things in advance. When you buy a car, you must maintain the car, or eventually, it will need repairs. You know you will have to do oil changes, change brake pads, rotors, etc. You don't know what may happen to your car that you didn't expect. It is the same with your house and your body. We know that without the proper attention, they will eventually break down. This is a very real problem for people who do not have a handle on their finances. A person who is living paycheck to paycheck cannot afford to entertain any surprises like the car breaking down or the water heater leaking or the air conditioner not working on the hottest day of summer. It is in our best interest to be as prepared as we can for the unexpected because something unexpected will happen.

If something happens the money has to come from somewhere and if you don't have an emergency fund established the first thing you are going to do is reach for the credit card. Beside the car, you have appliances that could break down, jobs that could lay you off or medical emergencies that could come up without any warning. Establishing an emergency fund to cover such predicaments as well as enough to cover several months of living expenses would be wise in case you become unemployed or unable to work.

You should also develop an investment

plan. The goal is to seek out ways to make your money, make more money. The best thing you can do is to find ways to have multiple streams of income, especially passive income like real estate, stocks, etc. If you pay yourself first, you will establish the habit of saving money for your future dreams, hopes, investments and unexpected expenses.

It is very important that you develop a retirement plan that will allow you to have the amount of money you need available when you retire. You have to plan and give a portion of your money towards retirement so that you can live a comfortable lifestyle when you decide to retire from your job. If you don't plan to set aside money and investments for your retired years, you may have to work longer because you can't afford to retire. To avoid this from happening to you, develop a retirement plan that will allow you to do whatever you want to do, especially, if you plan to start your own business when you leave your 9 to 5.

Don't take these steps all at once. Just like the steps of a stair, take them one step at a time. Get better at each of them and then add the next one as you go along. Remember, as I encouraged you at the beginning of the book, your current net worth has no comparison to your self-worth. You are valuable. This is something you can do, I believe in you. I'm here for you. I would love to work with you further.

If you would like further help getting unstuck and unlocking your money mindset so that you can get to your next level and experience financial freedom and success or if you desire to work with me in more detail on how to take authority over your money and keep more of what you earn, please go to:

http://www.saundragage.com

or If you would like to signup for my online courses please go to:

https://prosperous-living-academy.teachable.com

I look forward to hearing from you and being able to help you in this process.